Machiavelli
Renaissance Political Analyst and Author

MAKERS OF THE MIDDLE AGES AND RENAISSANCE

Machiavelli

Renaissance Political Analyst and Author

Heather Lehr Wagner

CHELSEA HOUSE
PUBLISHERS
A Haights Cross Communications Company ®
Philadelphia

COVER: Portrait of Niccolò Machiavelli, Casa del Machiavelli, Sant Andrea, in Percussina, Italy.

CHELSEA HOUSE PUBLISHERS
VP, NEW PRODUCT DEVELOPMENT Sally Cheney
DIRECTOR OF PRODUCTION Kim Shinners
CREATIVE MANAGER Takeshi Takahashi
MANUFACTURING MANAGER Diann Grasse

Staff for Machiavelli
EXECUTIVE EDITOR Lee Marcott
EDITORIAL ASSISTANT Carla Greenberg
PRODUCTION EDITOR Noelle Nardone
COVER AND INTERIOR DESIGNER Keith Trego
LAYOUT 21st Century Publishing and Communications, Inc.

A Haights Cross Communications ✦ Company ®

www.chelseahouse.com

First Printing

9 8 7 6 5 4 3 2 1

Library of Congress Cataloging-in-Publication Data

Wagner, Heather Lehr.
    Machiavelli : Renaissance political analyst and author/Heather Lehr Wagner.
        p. cm.–(Makers of the Middle Ages and Renaissance)
    Includes bibliographical references and index.
    ISBN 0-7910-8629-1 (hard cover)
    1. Machiavelli, Niccolò, 1469-1527–Juvenile literature. 2. Statesmen–Italy–
Florence–Biography–Juvenile literature. 3. Intellectuals–Italy–Florence–
Biography–Juvenile literature. 4. Florence (Italy)–History–1421-1737–Juvenile
literature. 5. Florence (Italy)–Biography–Juvenile literature. 6. Renaissance–
Italy–Florence–Juvenile literature. I. Title. II. Series.
    DG738.14.M2W29 2005
    320.1'092–dc22

                                                                2005007047

CONTENTS

Portrait of a Political Philosopher

During the earliest years of the sixteenth century, Italy was not a single unified country, but rather a collection of warring city-states, each forming alliances with other city-states or with outside powers to further its influence and control. As their homeland spun into political chaos, Italian philosophers and artists were revolutionizing the world with their great work. Governments revolved between monarchies and republics, wars were frequent, and tyrants quickly rose to power through skillful alliances and military might.

In an age in which the fate of a city-state—and the well-being of its citizens—rested on its ability to form useful alliances while thwarting invasions and attacks, diplomacy became a critical tool for survival. At this crucial time, diplomat Niccolò Machiavelli developed the theories and philosophies that would make him, for a brief period, one of the most significant political figures of the Renaissance.

More than 500 years after Machiavelli was born, his name is still recognized as a synonym for political ruthlessness, cunning, and even treachery and deceit. His writings in *The Prince*—shocking in their endorsement of an uncompromising willingness to do whatever necessary to retain power—offered his own formula for political policies that would ensure lasting governments.

Machiavelli was more than a ruthless political schemer. His ideas were based on solid observations, years of diplomacy, and the study of those he felt were highly successful political leaders.

Machiavelli's political theories, at times shocking, were based on solid observations, years of diplomacy, and the study of those he felt were the most successful political leaders.

During his lifetime, representing the powers in Florence, he met with King Louis XII and Emperor Maximilian. He studied the successful campaigns of Cesare Borgia, and traveled with Pope Julius II.

When the powerful Medici family regained control of Florence, Machiavelli was imprisoned and tortured. He spent most of the rest of his life attempting to recapture the power he had lost, courting the Medicis, and writing about politics and the history of Florence.

Machiavelli has been depicted as an evil advisor, a man who shaped his plans based not on what was best for the state or the people, but on ensuring that power remained in the control of the ruler he happened to be advising. While all of this may be true, Machiavelli—and his writings—must be understood in the context of the age in which he lived and wrote. The Italian city-states, including Machiavelli's own city-state of Florence, were in a nearly-constant state of political crisis during his lifetime, victims (Machiavelli believed) of incompetent rulers and the ambitions of foreign nations. Machiavelli's aim was to restore Florence to its former greatness, to protect it from invading and occupying armies, and to ensure its continued viability as an independent city-state. Sadly he would not succeed, but his political theories would bring him a great deal of acclaim.

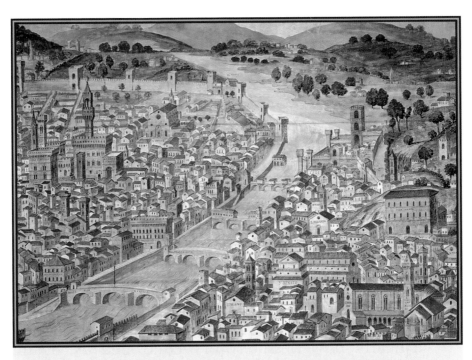

Machiavelli's own city-state of Florence was in a nearly constant state of political crisis during his lifetime. Machiavelli's aim was to restore Florence to its former greatness, to protect it from invading and occupying armies, and to ensure its continued viability as an independent city-state.

In order to understand Niccolò Machiavelli, to better understand why he wrote "what men do, and not what they ought to do," we must appreciate the world in which he lived.[1] Machiavelli was as much a product of the Renaissance as Michelangelo or Leonardo da Vinci. Like them, he focused on depicting new ways of viewing and understanding

the world. His art, however, was the "art of politics"—
the diplomatic skill of seizing and retaining power.
For Machiavelli, the Italy in which he lived was at a
critical crossroads, in desperate need of "someone to
save her from those barbarous cruelties," a country
eager and willing "to follow a banner, if only someone will raise it."[2]

A STATE IN DECLINE

Machiavelli witnessed the evolution of his native
Florence from a leading force in the Renaissance to
a nearly powerless territory controlled by Spain.
Growing up surrounded by the magnificence of
Florence's cathedrals, buildings, and public spaces—
and by the evidence of artistic accomplishment every-
where—Machiavelli was equally struck by the evidence
of Florence's diminished role in the world. On one
of his earliest diplomatic missions, to the court of
France's King Louis XII, Machiavelli was caught in
the embarrassing position of representing a city-state
whose idea of its own importance far exceeded the
reality of how it was viewed by the powers around
it. Florence was a city-state unable to respond
quickly or adopt a single position and stick to it.

Machiavelli quickly learned that military position and wealth, not past accomplishments, garnered respect in the diplomatic circles in which he was operating. His earliest diplomatic lessons showed that procrastination implied weakness. Boldness, both in politics and in war, was a critical factor in a city-state's ability to remain powerful in the eyes of its allies and foes.

Despite his cynical assessment of political realities, Machiavelli remained hopeful that Florence could recapture its lost glory. He believed that, by following certain basic precepts, Florentine leaders could once more seize power, to earn the respect of their people and of those who would threaten their sovereignty. In writing *The Prince*, Machiavelli believed that he was offering to Lorenzo de' Medici advice that could restore Florence to its former glory. He wrote:

> I have not found among my belongings anything as dear to me or that I value as much as my under-standing of the deeds of great men, won by me from a long acquaintance with contemporary affairs and a continuous study of the ancient world.[3]

The core aspects of Machiavelli's political theories were formed early, through the study of the successes

In writing his most famous work, *The Prince*, Machiavelli believed he was offering Lorenzo de' Medici (ruler of Florence, shown here) advice that could restore Florence to its former glory.

and failures of various powerful men he encountered on his diplomatic missions. Machiavelli believed that success came, not merely as a result of luck or intelligence, but in a critical combination of the two, when a man was wise enough to adapt his strategy to the times, and effectively master luck through skill and boldness. In a letter in 1506 to Giovan Battista Soderini, the nephew of one of his patrons, Machiavelli outlined the basis of his theory about the kind of leader who would ultimately triumph:

I believe that just as Nature has created men with different faces, so she has created them with different intellects and imaginations. As a result, each man behaves according to his own intellect and imagination. And, on the other hand, because times change and the pattern of events differs, one man's hopes may turn out as he prayed they would. The man who matches his way of doing things with the conditions of the times is successful; the man whose actions are at odds with the times and the pattern of events is unsuccessful. Hence, it can well be that two men can achieve the same goal by acting differently:

because each one of them matches his actions to what he encounters and because there are as many patterns of events as there are regions and governments. But because times and affairs often change—both in general and in particular—and because men change neither their imaginations nor their ways of doing things accordingly, it turns out that a man has good fortune at one time and bad fortune at another. And truly, anyone wise enough to adapt to and understand the times and the pattern of events would always have good fortune or would always keep himself from bad fortune; and it would come to be true that the wise man could control the stars and the Fates.[4]

SIDELINED BY POLITICS

Machiavelli's greatest flaw was, perhaps, the fact that he was much better at observing and advising than acting. Following a failed attempt to build a Florentine militia, which was soundly defeated by Spanish forces in 1512, Machiavelli was forced out of office when the Medici family returned to power. Machiavelli continued to study political events, but as an observer rather than as a participant. His observations would become clear in *The Prince, Discourses on the First Decade of Titus Livius,* and *The Art of War,* works that would continue to inspire debate and controversy nearly 500 years after they were written.

Machiavelli cared far less about who would rule his city-state than about that ruler's ability to form a strong government—a government capable of imposing unity, not merely in Florence, but in all of Italy. Machiavelli believed that city-states and nations must pass through cycles of prosperity and hardship, periods of greatness, and periods of conquest. Machiavelli hoped that a strong ruler could make the best of these cycles, turning a nation's fortune from bad to good through ruthless decision-making and decisive leadership.

Like the other artists of the Renaissance, Machiavelli challenged conventional thinking and sought to shape a new way of looking at the world. His view of politics as art offers a powerful commentary on how and why leaders behave the way they do. In *The Prince* and other writings, Machiavelli was not merely interested in serving as a historian—a recorder of the actions, successes, and failures of the leaders he had observed. His goal was to offer a powerful prescription for political power, to restore Florence and all of Italy to their former glory in the world.

Ultimately Machiavelli is best remembered for his argument that the rightness of political actions can only be judged in hindsight, once enough time has passed for future generations to determine what that action was meant to achieve, and assess whether or not the goal was achieved. The term *Machiavellian,* which has come to symbolize ruthlessness, is largely associated with politicians who seek to sacrifice the good of their nation in order to preserve their own power.

Machiavelli, however, was not really interested in preserving the power of a single man, or allowing a single dynasty to flourish and rule. His focus was on ensuring the success and continuation of Florence, no matter who its leader might be. His loyalty to Florence was more powerful than his loyalty to any one ruler, and his love for the city-state was formed from the time he was a boy.

Test Your Knowledge

1 Machiavelli's name is most often associated with
a. a philosophy of compassionate equality.
b. political ruthlessness and treachery.
c. the finest artists in sixteenth-century Italy
d. violent revolution and political upheaval.

2 Which of the following is true of the Italian city-states of Machiavelli's time?
a. They worked together to create a unified Italy.
b. They were conquered by the Spanish.
c. They were often engaged in petty wars and feuds.
d. None of the above

3 What did Machiavelli learn was most important for gaining respect in diplomatic circles?
a. Military position and wealth
b. Past accomplishments in the arts
c. Gaining the favor of the Catholic Church
d. A tradition of democratic government

4 How did Machiavelli believe that his work, *The Prince*, would be used?
a. As a plan to unify Europe
b. As a plan for the Medici family to increase their wealth
c. As a plan to help Italy to conquer other countries
d. As a plan for restoring Florence to its former greatness

5   What became of Machiavelli's plan to raise a
    Florentine militia?
    a. It succeeded and he became ruler of Florence.
    b. It failed and Machiavelli was forced from
       political office.
    c. The Spanish agreed to share joint rule over
       Florence.
    d. None of the above

ANSWERS: 1. b; 2. c; 3. a; 4. d; 5. b

Early Years
in Florence

Niccolò Machiavelli was born on May 3, 1469, in Florence, Italy. At the time of his birth, Florence was in the midst of a golden age, at a powerful point in its history. Thanks to the influence of Cosimo de' Medici, the untitled, unofficial political leader of Florence, the city-state had become a center for political activity.

15

Medici money had sponsored many of the leading artists whose creations were sparking a new movement—a "rebirth" in the arts—that would become known as the Renaissance. Cosimo de' Medici had died only a few years earlier, and his son Piero was now in power. Piero de' Medici was not the dynamic man that his father had been, but Florence's alliances still seemed strong. Its power was respected, and its artists were praised. Only a month after Niccolò Machiavelli entered the world, all of Florence would be invited to celebrate the wedding of Piero de' Medici's oldest son, Lorenzo, to Claire Orsini, the daughter of a noble Roman family. The celebration would last for days, and include glittering costumes, a jousting tournament, and endless feasting.

While the celebration marked a glorious chapter in Florence's history, young Niccolò Machiavelli's family was not directly impacted by the power and splendor of the ruling family. The Machiavellis were a respected Florentine family. Many of the Machiavelli men had played an important role in Florence's politics and held prestigious positions in its government, but Niccolò's father, Bernardo, was from a different branch of the family—a distinctly more middle-class branch. Bernardo Machiavelli was a lawyer, but not a very successful one. He was often mentioned as an intelligent man, but he had few clients. He was able to provide his family with enough money for food, and a comfortable—but not luxurious—home, but he was neither ambitious enough, nor hardworking enough, to provide much more.

Bernardo Machiavelli had one real passion: he loved books. Much of his money was spent to purchase a small but impressive personal library containing many of the important books of the day. He collected works by Greek and Roman philosophers, such as Cicero and Aristotle. He collected major studies of Italian history, and he collected important speeches that had been published, along with studies of military successes. These books would provide his son Niccolò with a foundation of knowledge about the ideas of noble Greek and Roman thinkers. Books would also provide Niccolò Machiavelli with a comprehensive understanding of the history of Italy, which would shape his own writing many decades later.

The Machiavelli family lived in a modest home on Via Guicciardini, just south of the Arno River, on a road that stretched from the Ponte Vecchio to the Pitti Palace. They also had a small home in the country. They were a family of six: Bernardo; his wife, Bartolomea; two daughters, Primavera and Margerita; Niccolò; and another son, Totto, born about six years after Niccolò.

In Florence in the fifteenth century, connections were the most important thing a man could offer his family. Hard work and ambition meant little. Those who were fortunate enough to be born into a wealthy and/or powerful family would enjoy the best Florence had to offer. Those with connections to these wealthy and powerful families would receive the best opportunities in business and in marriage.

The Machiavelli family had neither power nor powerful connections, but Niccolò still managed to receive a good education. The majority of what Niccolò Machiavelli learned, he read in books. He mastered Latin and read poetry. He learned basic grammar and how to use an abacus. He learned to write and to speak properly, studying the words of great speeches. He came to appreciate the verbal skill of great orators.

By the age of seven, he was walking through the streets of Florence to reach the homes of his teachers. At first, he was taught by Maestro Matteo, who received a monthly fee to train Niccolò in Latin grammar. Only a few months later, having exhausted all that Maestro Matteo could teach him, Niccolò Machiavelli walked more than half a mile each way to his new teacher, Ser Battista di Filippo da Poppi, who had a small school in a church, where Niccolò studied ancient Roman history.

By the time he was ten, Niccolò Machiavelli was studying arithmetic with yet another teacher, and, by the age of 12, a new teacher was instructing him in Latin. Later he also studied writing and music. Because his family could not afford a single prominent tutor or school, Niccolò moved from one teacher to another, absorbing all that each instructor could offer, before moving on to someone new.

Whatever these teachers could not provide, Niccolò Machiavelli could almost always find in the books of his father's library. He read Virgil, Ovid, and other Latin poets. He read Plutarch, Pliny, and Dante. He studied history, reading about the war between Sparta and Athens. He read of the great and corrupt leaders of the Roman Empire, and he studied the traits that marked the heroes of ancient Rome and Greece.

As he walked through the streets of Florence, he learned the history of his city, seeing the greatness of its noble architecture and the artistry of its sculpture. He listened as the people around him discussed politics. His school was not found in a single building; it was all around him.

THE GOLDEN CITY

In the late fifteenth century, Florence was a city that had emerged from the darkness of the Middle Ages into the light of the Renaissance. Great artists, such as Boticelli and Fra Angelico, were creating masterpieces under the sponsorship of the Medici family. The medieval walls of Florence still encircled a relatively small city. Magnificent churches and public buildings, however, provided evidence of the city's glory—not only of its glorious past, but also of what most believed would be its glorious future. The city was prosperous, thanks, in large part, to the success of its silk and woolens businesses. The Medici family that ruled Florence had made its fortune in banking, and the successful investments of the Medicis meant that Florence was wealthy, too. The Medici family's powerful connections brought diplomats, political leaders, even popes to the city, sparking a community deeply engaged in discussions of politics and philosophy.

Only a few months after Niccolò Machiavelli's birth, Piero de' Medici died, and his young son Lorenzo inherited the throne. Lorenzo de' Medici and his younger brother, Giuliano, were intelligent, talented, athletic young men, who loved spectacles and tournaments. In the first few years of Lorenzo de' Medici's reign, much of Florence enjoyed costume galas, spectacular balls, and brilliant displays of fireworks.

A plot to assassinate Lorenzo and Giuliano de' Medici would soon bring these carefree days to an end. On April 26, 1478, a group of conspirators attempted to kill Lorenzo and Giuliano de' Medici while they attended Mass at the Duomo, Florence's largest cathedral. The plot ended with the murder of Giuliano de' Medici. Lorenzo de' Medici escaped, but was wounded. Those involved in what would become known as the Pazzi Conspiracy—named

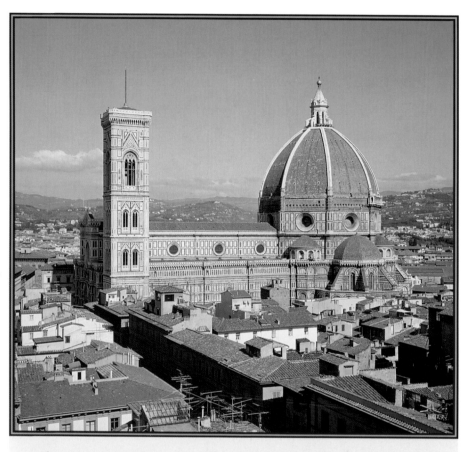

Only a few months after Niccolò Machiavelli's birth, Piero de' Medici died, and his young son Lorenzo inherited the throne as ruler of Florence. On April 26, 1478, a group of conspirators attempted to kill Lorenzo and Giuliano de' Medici while they attended Mass at the Duomo, Florence's largest cathedral (shown here).

after the Pazzi family, who had joined with Pope Sixtus IV and his relatives in attempting to murder the Medicis and take over Florence—were hunted down and forced into exile. Many of them, including an archbishop, were immediately hanged.

The Pazzi Conspiracy took place when Niccolò Machiavelli was only nine years old. All of Florence discussed the unexpected attack on the Medici brothers during Mass. The bodies of many of those involved were dragged through the streets by a furious mob. These events clearly impacted Niccolò Machiavelli. Years later, he would note that people were generally unwilling to overthrow a leader who—like Lorenzo de' Medici—was both powerful and generous. Even powerful and wealthy men— like those of the Pazzi family—could be defeated, however, by excessive ambition or simple bad luck.

Pope Sixtus IV responded to the hanging of his archbishop, and to the exposure of his involvement in the plot, by excommunicating all of Florence and forbidding all other city-states from engaging in trade with Florence. War quickly followed, and the pope enlisted the aid of the king of Naples in attacking Florence. The citizens of Florence suffered greatly until Lorenzo de' Medici was able to secretly travel to Naples, meet with the king, and negotiate a peace treaty. By March 1480, he had returned to

Florence as a hero, earning the new name "Lorenzo the Magnificent."

Niccolò Machiavelli spent his teenage years in a Florence that celebrated this victory and continuously honored the man who was responsible for it. Lorenzo de' Medici cemented his power, ensuring that no other attempt could be made to overthrow him, and the people of Florence supported him in this effort. The citizens of Florence apparently wanted no other leader. Lorenzo de' Medici was a symbol of Florence's power and its importance. Through his sponsorship of artists like Michelangelo and Leonardo da Vinci, Lorenzo de' Medici helped turn Florence into a center of artistic achievement. For those who were wealthy and important, there was no better place in the world to live.

THE RISE OF SAVONAROLA

At the same time, a Dominican friar named Girolamo Savonarola became an outspoken critic of the Medicis. Arriving in Florence in 1489, he quickly became a popular speaker. His fiery messages denounced the Medicis, forecasting doom and destruction for them and all of their followers.

Savonarola urged all citizens of Florence to repent for their sins, shun all luxury and excess, and adopt instead a more simple and modest life.

Savonarola attracted quite a following, as large crowds gathered to listen to his powerful sermons describing the coming doom. His message was most popular among Florence's poorer citizens—those whose taxes paid for the comfortable lifestyle of the wealthy. Savonarola declared that Florence's leader, Lorenzo the Magnificent, was responsible for all that was good and evil in the city—and, in Savonarola's view, there was far more evil than good in Florence. By 1491, he was openly denouncing Lorenzo de' Medici, declaring that Lorenzo the Magnificent needed to immediately repent or he would be swept from power.

Certainly, Niccolò Machiavelli, who by now would have been in his early 20s, was aware of the outspoken friar and his sermons criticizing Florence's leader, but Niccolò Machiavelli did not share Savonarola's beliefs. Machiavelli was not convinced that Florence's salvation lay in the act of people giving up all games, dancing, and pleasures to devote themselves to prayer and fasting. He never

Dominican friar Girolamo Savonarola became the most outspoken critic of the Medicis. He urged all citizens of Florence to repent for their sins, shun all luxury and excess, and adopt instead a simple and modest life.

became one of the popular priest's followers, although he did agree that the fate of a people was deeply dependent on the behavior of their ruler.

In 1491, Savonarola predicted that, within a year, Lorenzo de' Medici would die, and his prediction proved correct. On his deathbed, Lorenzo de' Medici sent for Savonarola to hear his confession. The priest appeared, but before he agreed to hear Lorenzo de' Medici's confession and offer repentance, he demanded three things. First he asked Lorenzo to admit his faith in God's mercy. Medici quickly agreed. Next Savonarola demanded that Lorenzo de' Medici repay any public funds he had used for his own expenses. Again Medici agreed. Finally Savonarola demanded that Lorenzo de' Medici restore full liberty to Florence, removing it from Medici control. This demand, Lorenzo de' Medici could not meet. Instead he turned his face to the wall. He died only a short while later, on April 8, 1492, bringing the rule of Lorenzo the Magnificent to an end.

Lorenzo de' Medici's greatest achievement would be best understood only after his death. Using skillful diplomacy, he had created a balance of power among Italy's five most dominant city-states: Florence, Naples, Milan, Venice, and the so-called "papal states"—the states under the direct rule of the pope—based in Rome. Lorenzo de' Medici had warned that the greatest threat to Florence would come, not from one of these five Italian city-states, but from a foreign power, some nation outside of Italy. His dire warning would prove to be prophetic.

THE FRENCH INVASION

In 1494, the powerful army of the French king, Charles VIII, began its march into Italy, seizing territory as it moved southward. The king's army was unlike any the Italian city-states had ever seen. Accustomed to fighting small battles with neighboring city-states, often using hired soldiers, the Italian city-states were not prepared for the well-trained, well-equipped, French army of some 60,000 men. This army had the best artillery in all of Europe, and fought using light, mobile cannons that fired iron, rather than stone balls.

Instead of joining forces to preserve the alliance that Lorenzo de' Medici had established, each Italian city-state panicked at the arrival of the French, and

The powerful army of the French king, Charles VIII, seized a great deal of territory in Italy. The troops, shown here, are entering Florence.

worried only about preserving its own interests. Florence was no exception. Florentine ruler Piero de' Medici, Lorenzo's son, possessed few of his father's political skills. As the French army neared Florentine territory, he rushed out to negotiate a peace treaty, which gave away Florence's most critical fortresses—those that guarded the northern and western frontiers—in order to secure peace with the French.

When the people of Florence learned that Piero de' Medici had given to the French the keys to Florence's security, they were outraged. Upon his

Lorenzo the Magnificent

During Machiavelli's earliest years, Florence was led by the dynamic member of the Medici family known as Lorenzo the Magnificent. Lorenzo de' Medici was not simply a skilled political figure. He was also a poet and a patron of the arts. He invited the great thinkers and artists of the day to his palaces, even taking in the young artist Michelangelo after discovering him at work in one of the Medici gardens.

Surviving an assassination attempt that took the life of his brother, and successfully negotiating an end to a bitter war with the armies of Naples and Pope Sixtus IV, Lorenzo de' Medici was able to consolidate his power. Despite choosing not to take an official title (to have himself named a prince or king), Lorenzo de' Medici still managed to dominate much of Florentine life through skillful alliances and masterful political acts. He created Florence's diplomacy, oversaw its government, and approved the establishment of schools, churches, and libraries. He met with foreign dignitaries and rulers, and he return, Piero de' Medici was greeted by a force of armed Florentines. He was forced to retreat to the temporary safety of his palace. Fearing for his life, he

approved the construction of new public buildings, often financing them with his own money.

In a family of skilled politicians, Lorenzo de' Medici is considered by many to be the most brilliant of all—the best statesman and the wisest judge of artistic talent. Lorenzo de' Medici nurtured many talented young artists, including Leonardo da Vinci. He understood that Florence's safety and integrity depended upon firm alliances with other Italian city-states, and he took steps to negotiate these alliances. He wisely feared the rise of the great European powers, such as France and Spain, sensing that their armies would soon threaten Florence.

Although Lorenzo de' Medici's son proved a weak and incapable heir, the Medicis would recapture power. Lorenzo de' Medici's legacy included more than a time of great prosperity and artistic achievement for Florence. Both his son and his nephew would become popes, and his great-granddaughter, Catherine de' Medici, would become queen of France.

soon fled Florence, and the 60-year rule of the Medicis in Florence came to an end.

The end of Medici rule did not spell freedom for Florence, however. The French army, no longer heeded by attacks from the Florentine fortresses, quickly marched into the city. The French king was leading the effort, clearly demonstrating that he saw himself not only as the cosigner of a peace treaty, but also as the conqueror of Florence. His army moved through the city, leaving chalk marks on the doors of the most magnificent homes, the ones they intended to occupy. Niccolò Machiavelli later wrote of this in *The Prince*, noting that, "Charles the king of France was allowed to take Italy with chalk."[5]

In a humiliating period of Florentine history, thousands of French and Swiss soldiers marched into the city. Finally, a new agreement was reached with King Charles VIII. Florence agreed to pay him a large amount of cash and support him in his campaign to defeat Naples. In exchange, the French king agreed to pull his forces out of the city.

Even after the French troops withdrew, the city of Florence remained in chaos. The people of Florence were united on few points, although most agreed that they did not want the Medicis to return to power. Savonarola, in his sermons, spoke of the need for a "universal and civil way of living," a government in which the people of Florence were active participants.[6]

By 1494, Florence had been shaped into a new republic, governed by the Grand Council (*Consiglio Grande*). Formation of the council had been Savonarola's idea, but this very council would betray the friar only four years later. By 1498, Savonarola's charges of corruption no longer focused on Florence's ruling elite. Instead he targeted the corruption that he claimed existed throughout the Roman Catholic Church. The pope sent an envoy to Florence, demanding that Savonarola be investigated on charges of heresy—spreading opinions contrary to the teachings of the Catholic Church—and the council complied. On May 24, 1498, Girolamo Savonarola was hanged in the plaza outside the council's meeting place. Only four days later, Niccolò Machiavelli's political career began.

Test Your Knowledge

1 Machiavelli's father was
   a. a librarian.
   b. a lawyer.
   c. a prince.
   d. a banker.

2 Which of the following did Machiavelli learn
   was most important for acquiring power?
   a. Family connections
   b. Hard work and ambition
   c. A respect for the arts
   d. Devotion to the Catholic Church

3 The young Machiavelli received his education
   from
   a. a series of teachers.
   b. his father's books.
   c. long walks through the streets of Florence.
   d. all of the above.

4 Dominican friar Savonarola challenged Lorenzo
   de' Medici because
   a. he believed in a democratic form of government.
   b. he believed that excessive wealth and luxury
      were sinful.
   c. he resented Machiavelli's friendship with
      Lorenzo de' Medici.
   d. none of the above.

5 How did the Italian city-states react to the invasion
   by France in 1494?
   a. They joined together to defeat the French.
   b. They discovered a way to destroy the French
      artillery.
   c. They panicked, tried to fight the French
      separately, and lost.
   d. They appealed to the papal army for help.

ANSWERS: 1. b; 2. a; 3. d; 4. b; 5. c

Diplomatic Career

Machiavelli owed his political appointment, at least in part, to Girolamo Savonarola's fall from grace. As Savonarola faced charges of heresy, many of those in the Florentine government who had been the friar's supporters and followers were dismissed from their positions. One of those dismissed was Alessandro

Girolamo Savonarola's claims of corruption in the Catholic Church caused him to be investigated on charges of heresy, a crime punishable by death. He was found guilty, and, on May 24, 1498, he was hanged in the plaza outside the council's meeting place. His demise probably helped Machiavelli gain his first government position.

Braccesi, who had been head of the Second Chancery, a government office charged with handling foreign affairs and diplomacy. Niccolò Machiavelli was barely 29 years old when he was nominated as Braccesi's replacement. Machiavelli had no political experience, but his nomination was approved—perhaps because he was known not to be a supporter of Savonarola. He was confirmed by the Grand Council on June 19, 1498.

Employees of the Second Chancery were expected to be skilled diplomats, and to be scholars—familiar with Latin, talented at using language, knowledgeable about the classics, and familiar with ancient history and philosophy. Machiavelli possessed all of these qualities, perhaps explaining how an unknown young man with no prior experience was able to head the Second Chancery so quickly. Machiavelli was well versed in all of the required subjects, and some reports suggest that he had studied the classics at the University of Florence. His mentor at the university was Marcello Adriani, who would later become the first secretary of the Republic of Florence. Perhaps Adriani had even helped to place one of his most talented students in his first government position.

Regardless of how he got there, as head of the Second Chancery, Machiavelli was quickly charged with serving as secretary to the Florentine commission that oversaw military and foreign affairs, known as the Ten of Liberty and Peace. (Ironically, the commission was also known as the Ten of War.) His responsibilities included keeping the commission members informed of political and military problems, and providing them with the information they would need to make decisions about Florence's foreign policy. His job also involved traveling, in order to report on foreign affairs.

EARLIEST DIPLOMATIC EFFORTS

Machiavelli's earliest missions immediately tested his diplomatic skills. On his first mission, in March 1499, he was sent to visit Jacopo d'Appiano, lord of Piombino, a port town near the island of Elba. Jacopo d'Appiano had been hired by Florentine officials to help in the war against Pisa. Now he was demanding more money for his soldiers. Machiavelli's mission was to inform d'Appiano that he could not have more money for his soldiers, but 40 more soldiers were needed to join those already fighting. Machiavelli's challenge was to deliver the bad news in words so broad and general that d'Appiano would remain convinced that Florence was still his ally.

Only four months later, Machiavelli had yet another tricky mission, this one again involving payment for a hired army. In July 1499, Machiavelli was sent to call upon Caterina Sforza in her castle in Forlì, a town northwest of Florence. Sforza was a powerful and beautiful woman whose son Ottaviano had been hired by Florence to help in the war against Pisa. Like d'Appiano, he wanted more money, and was refusing to agree to fight for another year, unless his salary was increased to match an offer by the Duke of Milan.

Machiavelli did his best to persuade Caterina Sforza to offer her son's support for another year, but she wanted something more than mere words. She wanted acts that would guarantee Florence's protection of her land, which was being threatened by the army of the illegitimate son of Pope Alexander VI, an ambitious young man named Cesare Borgia. She demanded a commitment in writing, which Florence was not prepared to give.

In the end, Machiavelli left without Caterina Sforza's support, and she did not have Florence's protection when Cesare Borgia's army invaded Forlì. She bravely remained in her home until the end,

Caterina Sforza was a powerful and beautiful woman whose son Ottaviano had been hired by Florence to help in the war against Pisa. In July 1499, Machiavelli called upon Caterina Sforza in her castle in Forlì, a town northwest of Florence. He was seeking her help in the effort to keep her son fighting against Pisa.

when she was finally seized by Borgia's army and sent off to become a prisoner of the pope. Nonetheless the woman responsible for the failure of one of

Caterina Sforza

One of Machiavelli's earliest diplomatic missions took him to Forlì, to negotiate with Caterina Sforza and obtain the military support of her son Ottaviano. Ottaviano Sforza wanted more money, but Florence did not want to offer it. Caterina Sforza also had another goal: to secure the protection of Florence against what she feared was an imminent attack by Cesare Borgia. In the end, the mission failed and none of the three received what they wanted. Caterina Sforza's fears proved valid. Forlì was invaded by the army of Borgia, and she was seized as prisoner.

In *History of Florence*, Machiavelli praised Caterina Sforza for her courage during an earlier attack that had left her widowed. After assassins killed her husband, Count Girolamo, and threw his head out of a window, they seized Countess Caterina and her children:

> Only the fortress was left to take, if their attempt was to succeed. Since the castellan would not give it up, they asked the Countess

his earliest diplomatic missions had made a great impression upon Machiavelli. He cited her courage in several of his later published works, including

to influence him. This she promised to do, if they would let her enter the fortress; as a pledge of her faith, they were to retain her children. The conspirators believed her talk and allowed her to enter. When she was inside, she threatened them with death and with every sort of punishment in revenge for her husband. When they threatened to kill her children, she answered that she had with her means for producing more. Then the conspirators became terrified, for they were not supported by the Pope and they heard that Signor Lodovico Sforza, the Countess' uncle, was sending men to aid her; so they took such property as they could carry and went to Città di Castello. Then the Countess, reassuming power, with every sort of cruelty revenged her husband's death.*

* Niccolò Machiavelli, *The History of Florence, Book 8*, in *Machiavelli: The Chief Works and Others, Vol. 3*. Durham, NC: Duke University Press, 1989, pp. 1430–1431.

Discourses, Florentine Histories, The Art of War, The Prince, and the history of Italy known as *First Decennial.*

MISSION TO FRANCE

The diplomatic skills that Machiavelli had developed were desperately needed when, in July 1500, he was sent to France, to the court of King Louis XII. Accompanying Francesco della Casa, an ambassador, Machiavelli's task was a difficult one. France had agreed to aid Florence in its war with Pisa, and had sent a military force to help the Florentines, but the soldiers Florence had hired quickly deserted during the siege of Pisa. Swiss soldiers provided by the French also deserted because they had not been paid. The attack had to be called off, resulting in embarrassment for all involved. The king of France wanted to make it clear that France was not responsible for the defeat. Machiavelli's mission from Florence, meanwhile, was to explain that the disaster was not the fault of Florence, but, instead, was due to the corrupt and cowardly actions of the French commander.

Machiavelli and Francesco della Casa spent the next six months attempting to negotiate with King

Louis XII, and during that time, Machiavelli received one of his most important lessons in politics. On his earlier missions, he had been serving as a representative to small territories allied with Florence. He had, in a sense, been representing the mightier power, and negotiating from a position of strength. In the court of France, his experience was totally different. It was evident in the attitudes of all of the French royals, from the king downward, that Florence, in their eyes, was a small and insignificant player in politics—a republic whose incompetence was evident in its ongoing, unsuccessful war with Pisa. Machiavelli was forced to report to the Florentine legislature that the French "only value those who are well-armed or willing to pay." France believed that "both these qualities are lacking in your case."[7]

The situation grew worse, as the French demanded repayment of the money they had spent on the Swiss troops at Pisa, as well as support for the ongoing maintenance of the French army in Italy. Francesco della Casa became ill in mid-September and left the negotiations solely to Machiavelli. He was now in the embarrassing position of not actually being an ambassador—the only one who was actually qualified to renegotiate the treaty with the French. For months, Machiavelli promised that the arrival of the Florentine ambassadors would be imminent, and yet he was continually embarrassed by their failure to arrive. Finally, in December 1500, the ambassadors arrived and Machiavelli was able to return to Florence. His father had died shortly before his departure for France, and his sister had died while he was in France. Throughout his time in France, he had been confronted by the clear evidence that Florence mattered little on the world stage. Indeed Florence's own sense of importance was far greater than it deserved.

THE RISE OF CESARE BORGIA

Machiavelli returned to a lonely family home. His father and sister were gone and his mother had died in 1496. Only his brother remained in the house, and Machiavelli began to long for a more animated family atmosphere. He dated, and then married, a young woman named Marietta Corsini, in 1501.

Marriage did not prevent Machiavelli from pursuing other women. It seems, however, that Machiavelli's long absences from home, due to business travel, rather than his romancing of other women, were most troublesome to his wife. She wrote to him often, begging for news as he traveled on various diplomatic missions. In one letter, she informed him of the birth of their son, stating:

> For now the baby is well, he looks like you: he is white as snow, but his head looks like black velvet, and he is hairy like you. Since he looks like you, he seems beautiful to me. And he is so lively he seems to have been in the world for a year; he opened his eyes when he was scarcely born and filled the whole house with noise.[8]

By 1501, Machiavelli was becoming increasingly aware of the growing threat of Cesare Borgia, the same Borgia who had threatened Caterina Sforza. In April 1501, Borgia was named Duke of Romagna by Pope Alexander VI. Borgia immediately responded by attacking neighboring territories in order to increase the size of his holdings.

Tall and handsome, with bright blue eyes, Cesare Borgia was an impressive figure when Machiavelli first met him in 1502. Borgia had earned a reputation for ruthlessness. Rumors suggested that he had murdered his brother and his brother-in-law, as well as countless other rivals. The pope named him commander-in-chief of his papal army. Borgia counted among his allies the king of France, and had been granted yet another title, Duke of Valentinois— earning him the nickname Valentino—by the time Machiavelli's mission led him to Borgia's court. Their first meeting added to the sense of mystery and fear surrounding Borgia. He welcomed Machiavelli to a meeting at night, allowing only a single candle to be lit in the room. Borgia was visible only dimly, as a tall shadow in the dark, clad in black.

Borgia informed Machiavelli of his friendship with and support of Florence, noting that it would be wise for the Florentines to use him as their ally. At the same time, however, Borgia's soldiers warned Machiavelli that Borgia was an impatient man. He might enlist the aid of France in an attack on Florence. All he had to do was send word and an army would quickly appear, poised to attack Florence.

Machiavelli later witnessed Borgia putting down a revolt by some of his captains. As the soldiers prepared to riot, Borgia invited their leaders to a meeting, offering them fine food and wine, and

In April 1501, Cesare Borgia (shown here) was named Duke of Romagna by Pope Alexander VI. Borgia had earned a reputation for ruthlessness, and was suggested to have murdered his brother and his brother-in-law, as well as other rivals.

promising them his continued support. As the men relaxed, Borgia's hidden guards jumped out, seizing and murdering the rebellious captains.

To Machiavelli, this display was evidence of Borgia's superior skills as a leader. Reporting to the members of the Ten of War on what he had seen—observations that would later be echoed in *The Prince*—Machiavelli noted that Borgia should be regarded as a rising power in Italy, someone who "made use of every means and action possible" for "putting down his roots" and was busy laying "mighty foundations for future power."[9]

While Machiavelli admired Borgia's self-confidence, decisiveness, and courage—all qualities that he would later note were critical for successful leadership—he was unsettled by evidence that Borgia had benefited from extraordinary luck in many of his campaigns. In October 1503, Machiavelli was sent on a mission to Rome, where he would again encounter Borgia, this time under a very different set of circumstances.

Many of Borgia's earliest campaigns had been funded and supported by his father, Pope Alexander VI. Only two months before Machiavelli's arrival in Rome, the pope had died, and his successor, Pope Pius II, had died one month later. Machiavelli was sent to determine who the next pope would be. Concern was spreading throughout Florence that the new pope would be Cardinal Giuliano della Rovere, a man who was known to have close ties to the Medicis, and who might possibly, as pope, help to restore them to power in Florence.

Borgia was in Rome, too, and soon announced his personal support for the choice of Rovere as the new pope. In exchange, Borgia had been promised a position as captain-general of the pope's armies. Soon after Rovere's election as pope, he took the new name Pope Julius II. Clearly Borgia had made an error in choosing to support Rovere. Borgia's father, Alexander VI, had despised Rovere, and had forced him into exile for ten years. While Borgia might have forgotten this incident, it quickly became clear that Rovere had not. Borgia never received his appointment to serve as head of the pope's armies, and as he waited in vain, the people living in his territories, who had long been terrorized by Borgia, suddenly realized that the power and authority Borgia had received when his father was pope no longer existed. He did not have a papal army to command and soon his people began to revolt.

Machiavelli watched in disgust as Borgia continued to wait for his luck to turn, his supporters slipped away, and his lands fell out of his control. He soon reported to the Ten of War that Borgia was no longer a threat. The pope had him arrested and Machiavelli noted in one of his dispatches back to Florence, ". . . it seems that this Duke little by little is slipping into his grave. . . ." [10]

MILITARY REFORM

While Machiavelli harshly judged Borgia for his over-reliance on good luck and family connections, he remained an admirer of the duke's courage and, perhaps more important, his wise use of an army that he had built himself. Rather than following the practice of hiring mercenary soldiers, who were often undisciplined and unmotivated, Borgia had created his army, using men from his own land.

Machiavelli believed that Florence needed to adopt a similar model for its militia, and for several years, as the war with Pisa dragged on, he repeatedly made his argument to his superiors. As the war with Pisa slipped into its twelfth year, fought ineptly by a series of poorly paid armies, Machiavelli's proposal for a militia began to make more sense. The biggest objections were the fears, on the part of some Florentines, that a single individual in charge of Florence's militia might be able to gain control of Florence itself, seizing power, and forming a military dictatorship.

Finally Machiavelli received approval to form a small, "test" army, and he quickly got to work, drafting men and setting up a system to train them. He did all of this in addition to carrying out his regular duties, serving almost simultaneously as secretary of defense and as one of Florence's chief diplomats.

By February 1506, the members of the new Florentine militia were trained and ready, showing off their skills in a series of military parades, to the delight of the cheering crowds. Support for the militia grew so much that, by December 1506, a new department had been created within the government. Nine men would serve as magistrates for the militia, and Machiavelli was appointed as their chancellor.

Despite his obvious military successes, Machiavelli still had diplomatic duties to perform. In fact, in 1506, he was forced to leave the militia to travel to a meeting with Pope Julius II. The pope was attempting to retake the former papal city-states of Bologna and Perugia, and he was demanding Florence's help.

Test Your Knowledge

1   To what event did Machiavelli most owe his
first political appointment?
a. The death of the pope
b. A favor from a friend
c. The discrediting of Savonarola
d. None of the above

2   Which of the following were Machiavelli's
duties as head of the Second Chancery?
a. Keeping the chancery informed of political
and military problems
b. Making economic and trade policy
c. Declaring war on other city-states
d. Conferring with the pope

3   What can be said of Machiavelli's diplomatic
missions?
a. They turned him against politics.
b. They sharpened his negotiating skills.
c. They enabled the French to conquer Italy.
d. None of the above

4   Which of the following best describes
Cesare Borgia?
a. He was a patient and compassionate leader.
b. He was a ruthless power-seeker.
c. He gave Machiavelli his first job in politics.
d. He was a short and unattractive man.

5   Who was Cesare Borgia's father?

a. Pope Alexander VI

b. Pope Julius II

c. Machiavelli's second cousin

d. A poor peasant

ANSWERS: 1. c; 2. a; 3. b; 4. b; 5. a

Decline of the Republic

Machiavelli arrived at the court of Pope Julius II with one clear instruction—stall for time. The pope wanted Florence's assistance—and its hired troops— to attack Bologna. Florence needed its troops for the ongoing war with Pisa, but its leaders did not want to alienate the pope, who might then decide to attack the city of Florence.

Machiavelli seized the opportunity to study first-hand a man who was becoming one of Italy's most powerful forces. The pope had declared that he was on a crusade, a mission to drive all "barbarians" out of Italy. Machiavelli was astonished at the ease with which Pope Julius II backed up those grandiose words, staging skillful military campaigns, and quickly seizing control of Perugia and Bologna.

What impressed Machiavelli most was the idea that different men could behave very differently, and still be very successful leaders. The skills that seemed necessary for leadership seemed to vary, depending on the times and the people involved. Machiavelli was fascinated by the concept that a leader like Borgia might seize and hold power through cruelty and fear, while a leader like Lorenzo de' Medici remained strong and supported because of his skill at dispensing favors and earning the love of his people. Some rulers succeeded by building fortresses, while some—like Pope Julius II—gained support by using their religious beliefs as justification for their actions.

Machiavelli was beginning to understand a concept that would form the core of much of his political philosophy. In his view, a man's success or failure depended on whether his talents and imagination, and his actions, were well suited to the times and events.[11] In other words, different types of behavior, and different kinds of leadership, could result in a strong and powerful ruler. Machiavelli understood, however, that the key for a ruler to maintain power was in his ability to adapt to shifting attitudes and different settings. The same behavior will not succeed forever. The successful leader must be able to change his actions to suit different times.

EMPEROR MAXIMILIAN

Machiavelli's growing philosophy of leadership benefited from the opportunity to study yet another powerful man, Holy Roman Emperor Maximilian. In 1507, Maximilian announced his plans to march into Italy and have himself crowned in Rome by Pope Julius II. Emperor Maximilian had requested Florentine financial support for his campaign. Machiavelli was sent to determine whether or not the emperor was actually going to show up.

When Emperor Maximilian did, in fact, arrive, Machiavelli was not impressed. He found the emperor to be indecisive and easily influenced by the opinions of others. Machiavelli wrote about his perceptions in *The Prince*, when he stated that one of Maximilian's own men suggested that the emperor:

> gets advice from nobody and that he never in anything acts as he wishes to. . . . The Emperor is a secretive man, does not impart his plans to a soul, does not get any opinion on them. But when as they are put into effect they become generally known, they are at once opposed by those around him, and he, being pliable, is pulled away from them. Consequently, what he does one day he destroys the next; no one ever knows what he wishes or intends to do, and on his decisions it is impossible to rely.[12]

Machiavelli did, however, find one thing to admire during his mission to meet Maximilian. The Hapsburg court in Germany was impressive for its military organization. The soldiers were armed and well trained, and each city had armories containing weapons and munitions. In addition, a stockpile of

CLEOPHAS · FRATER · CARNALIS · IO:
SEPHI · MARITI · DIVAE · VIRG · MARIE ·

IACOBVS · MINOR · EPVS ·   MARIA · CLEOPHÆ · SOROR
HIEROSOLIMITANVS ·   VIRG · MAR · PVTATIVA · MA·
TERTERA · D · N

Holy Roman Emperor Maximilian II is shown here with his family. Machiavelli was not impressed by Emperor Maximilian. In fact, Machiavelli found the emperor to be indecisive and easily influenced by the opinions of others. Machiavelli wrote about his impressions in *The Prince*.

food and firewood was always available to help a city survive a siege, even one that might last for a year or more.

AN END TO THE WAR

Finally Machiavelli was able to test his militia in the war with Pisa, and he was right in the thick of the action when peace finally came in June 1509. He was one of the two signers of the document marking Pisa's official surrender. Machiavelli was widely praised for his role in the end to the lengthy war. Florence celebrated the victory, and much of the credit was given to Machiavelli, but the triumph would prove short-lived.

Pope Julius II was once more engaged in a campaign to drive the French from Italy, and his success would pose a great threat to Florence. The pope was openly allied with members of the Medici family, who were anxious to reestablish their rule over Florence and bring an end to the republic. The head of the Medici family, Giovanni de' Medici, was a cardinal who had demonstrated great acts of charity in Rome. Many Florentines were beginning to look upon him with favor, rather than viewing him as a threat to their liberty.

Florence was caught in a difficult spot. The French king's armies had asked Florence for aid, thus ensuring French support, and making it more

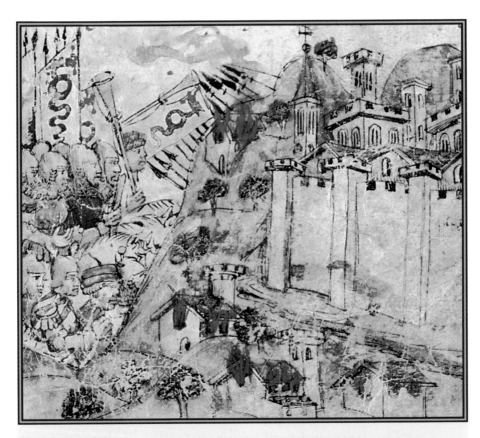

The conquest of Pisa is shown here. Machiavelli was able to test his militia during this war. He was also one of the two signers of the document marking Pisa's official surrender.

difficult for Pope Julius II's army. Openly aiding the French king, however, would certainly make Florence a target for the pope, and the pope's armies were much closer to Florence than the French army.

Machiavelli was given the challenging diplomatic mission of trying to forge an agreement between the pope and the French king. He arrived in France in July 1510, charged with the task of convincing the French king that, while Florence was its strong ally, maintaining a good relationship with the pope was critical. Finally Machiavelli was instructed to tell the French king, "not to break off relations with the pope; because if the pope is not worth much as a friend, as an enemy the pope can do great harm."[13]

Machiavelli's advice, after meeting with the king, was to attempt to arrange a peaceful arrangement between France and the pope. Each side had much to lose in a battle, and Machiavelli believed that Florence could act as an intermediary to help both sides save face.

The pope refused to listen to the diplomats from Florence. Worse still, he accused Florentine officials of obstructing his efforts to free Italy from the French, and threatened them. When Machiavelli returned to Florence, in late October 1510, he discovered that his native city was full of rumors and apprehension. The people of Florence were split between supporters of the Medicis and supporters of the republic. A plot was uncovered, involving a threat to the life of the *gonfalonier*, Florence's leading government official.

Machiavelli's family had grown to include five children, and eventually he would have six, but his political responsibilities left little time to spend with his wife and children

Machiavelli knew that the pope and the king of France would soon be at war. The unrest in Florence worried him. He sensed that the city could soon become a battleground, but those in the government were more concerned with maintaining their increasingly feeble grasp on power than with putting plans in place to help the city survive an attack. Machiavelli focused on his militia, inspecting the fortresses, recruiting additional soldiers, and parading and training his troops, but the troops were inexperienced. They had few trained commanders who had experience in war.

In October 1511, Pope Julius II established the Holy League, an alliance with Ferdinand, the king of Aragon, Venice, and Ferrara. In November, King Henry VIII of England joined the Holy League, and Emperor Maximilian joined shortly after. In the early skirmishes, France was victorious, but the death of its greatest captain shook the French army, and they quickly retreated. The Holy League's

armies swept south through Italy; first Milan, then
Bologna, Piacenza, and Parma fell. The pope was
emerging victorious, and he would soon turn his
attention to Florence.

A secret Holy League meeting was held in July
1512, to decide the fate of Florence. The gonfalonier
would be forced to resign. The republican government would be dissolved and the Medici family
would be brought back to power.

An army of Spanish soldiers, under the direction
of Pope Julius II, set up camp outside Prato, part
of Florentine territory. Only a small portion of the
Florentine militia had been sent to guard Prato.
The remainder was kept in Florence. As the walls
of Prato quickly fell to the Spanish onslaught, the
inexperienced Florentine militia panicked and ran.
Homes were burned, and the residents were tortured
and killed. More than 4,000 people were killed in
the violence.

The survivors made their way to Florence. As
they recounted what had happened, the people of
Florence began to panic. The gonfalonier, fearing for
his life, had fled the city during the night. Florence
was left without a leader.

In October 1511, Pope Julius II established the Holy League, an alliance with Ferdinand, the king of Aragon, Venice, and Ferrara. The pope, who was emerging victorious in battle, would soon turn his attention to Florence.

FALL OF THE REPUBLIC

Learning of the gonfalonier's hasty departure, supporters of the Medicis urged the people of Florence to revolt. A message was quickly dispatched to the pope's forces, expressing the willingness of the people to allow the Medicis to return. On September 1, 1512, the sons of Lorenzo de' Medici—Giovanni and Giuliano—and their cousin Giulio (accompanied by their nephew, Pietro's son Lorenzo), rode back into Florence. They were welcomed by enthusiastic crowds of cheering Florentines. The people had grown tired of the years of chaos, and remembered well the glory days that Florence had experienced under Medici rule. These three members of the Medici family had fled Florence as young men of 18, 16, and 15, respectively. They were now mature men of 36, 34, and 33.

The Medicis quickly seized power, aided by the presence of armed Spanish soldiers, and those who had served the former government were forced from office. On November 7, 1512, Machiavelli joined the ranks of the newly unemployed public servants in Florence. He had made an attempt to stay in office, writing to Cardinal Giovanni de'

Medici twice to offer his advice and service, but there was no reply. Instead Machiavelli was fired and banished from Florence three days later, with a warning to remain outside the city—but within Florentine territory. Ten days later, another letter informed Machiavelli that he was banned from entering the legislative palace where he had worked for the past year.

The final punishment was not completely carried out—in fact, Machiavelli was eventually ordered to return to the palace, but only to report to an investigative committee looking into the large sums of money given to Machiavelli to fund his militia. No charges were filed and Machiavelli was vindicated by the investigation, but after 14 years of service, he was without work, and soon his life would become even worse.

In February 1513, two young conspirators, plotting to assassinate the Medicis, put together a list of 20 people who might be willing to support them in their efforts. Machiavelli's name was on that list, and then the conspirators lost the list, which was quickly discovered by officials of the new government. Machiavelli was ordered to appear, to answer

The Return of the Medicis

Machiavelli was an astute observer of the world around him, and many of his observations were recorded in his letters and other published works. In a letter dated September 1512, sent from Florence to an unidentified woman, Machiavelli described the restoration of the Medici family to power in Florence:

> . . . The magnificent Medici . . . preferred not to come to Florence, unless first they settled the affairs of the city with the Vicar, with whom after some difficulties they made an agreement; and entering Florence, they were received by all the people with the utmost honor. There was established meanwhile in Florence a certain new order of government, in which it did not seem to the Vicar [the Viceroy, or head of the Spanish army] that there was security for the house of Medici or for the League; therefore he indicated to the Signors of the city that it was necessary to put the government in the form it had during the lifetime of the Magnificent Lorenzo. The noble citizens wished to accede to this, but feared that the multitude would not join in, and while they were carrying on this debate on how they would deal

with these things, the Legate entered Florence and with His Lordship came many soldiers and especially Italians. And the Signors of the city brought many citizens together in the Palace on the sixteenth day of the present month—and with them was the Magnificent Giuliano—and while they were talking about reform of the government, they heard a commotion in the Public Square, and Ramazzotto with his soldiers and others immediately seized the Palace, shouting: "Palle, palle." [a rallying cry referencing the symbol of the Medici family] And at once the whole city was under arms, and through every part of the city resounded that name, so that the Signors were obliged to summon the people to an assembly, which we call a parliament, where a law was passed by which the magnificent Medici were reinstated in all the honors and ranks of their ancestors. And this city remains very quiet, and hopes not to live less honored with their aid than she lived in times gone by, when the Magnificent Lorenzo their father, of most happy memory, was ruling.*

* Allan Gilbert, ed. *The Letters of Machiavelli.* New York: Capricorn Books, 1961, pp. 95–96.

for his alleged role in the assassination attempt. He was then put in prison, and tortured, in order to force him to confess.

Machiavelli had nothing to confess. He was held in chains in the dark, cold prison, listening as the leaders of the conspiracy were led to their deaths. His freedom came with the death of Pope Julius II on March 11, 1513. The newly elected pope was Giovanni de' Medici, and all of Florence rejoiced at the news of the election of the very first Florentine pope. Secure in their support, the Medicis decided to offer pardons to those who had been named in the conspiracy, and by March 12, Machiavelli was released from prison.

ATTEMPT TO WIN FAVOR

Only days after his release from prison, Machiavelli wrote to Frencesco Vettori, Florence's ambassador to the newly elected Medici pope, now known as Leo X. Describing Pope Leo X as "our Lord," Machiavelli pleaded for another chance to serve:

I won't go over again the long story of my misfortune, but will merely say that Luck has done everything to cause me this trouble. Yet, thanks be to God! it is over. I hope I won't run into it again, both because I shall be more careful and because the times will be more liberal and not so suspicious. . . . Keep me, if it is possible, in our Lord's memory, so that, if it is possible, he or his family may employ me in something or other, because I believe I would bring honor to him and profit to myself.[14]

Seven years would pass before Machiavelli would again receive an official commission. He would never, however, recapture the glory he had experienced during his exciting days as Florence's chief diplomat.

Test Your Knowledge

1   What problem did Machiavelli face in his meeting
    with Pope Julius II?
    a. If Florence spared troops to aid the
       pope against Bologna, it risked losing
       its battle against Pisa.
    b. Florence could not risk offending
       the pope.
    c. Machiavelli needed a way to stall the
       pope's request for aid.
    d. All of the above

2   In observing Pope Julius II, what quality
    did Machiavelli discover to be essential for
    long-term leadership?
    a. Ruthlessness
    b. Adaptability
    c. Physical strength
    d. Strong alliances

3   Which of the following did Machiavelli do
    during the war between Florence and Pisa?
    a. He went into hiding.
    b. He raised a militia and served admirably
       in battle.
    c. He served as economic advisor, but not
       military leader.
    d. He was killed in combat.

4 What was the Holy League?

  a. A group of renegade soldiers

  b. A nickname for Machiavelli's militia

  c. An alliance of forces formed by Pope Julius II

  d. None of the above

5 After the Spanish-backed Medici family regained power over Florence, Machiavelli was

  a. fired from his post.

  b. banished from the city.

  c. investigated for money given to his militia.

  d. all of the above.

ANSWERS: 1. d; 2. b; 3. b; 4. c; 5. d

The Prince

Machiavelli soon understood that his career in politics was over, at least for the immediate future. He had been told to leave Florence, and he had no great desire to stay as a helpless observer from the sidelines, while others managed the political actions without him.

When Machiavelli was told to leave Florence, he decided to move to Sant Andrea in Percussina, to the house his father had left him in the country. Once there, he began to write *The Prince.* His writing desk is shown here.

Machiavelli decided to move to Sant Andrea in Percussina, to the house his father had left him in the country. There he would be removed from the politics of Florence and would have the opportunity to focus on reading, studying, and thinking—but these were not pastimes that appealed to a man who had been actively involved in shaping Florence's politics for so many years. He quickly became restless, waking early, overseeing the cutting of wood from the forest on his land to sell it. When he met travelers along the road, he would ask for their local news. He often lunched with his wife and children before walking to a nearby inn to play games. He would spend evenings alone, in his study, reading history and analyzing the actions and words of kings and leaders of ages past.

Finally Machiavelli began to put down on paper his thoughts about these leaders of the past, coupled with analysis of the leaders he had been able to personally meet and observe in action. These observations and analyses became a booklet known as *The Prince*, and, at first, Machiavelli hoped to use it to prove his usefulness to the Medici family. He wrote to his friend and benefactor Francesco Vettori on December 10, 1513:

[I have] composed a little work *On Princedoms*, where I go as deeply as I can into considerations on this subject, debating what a princedom is, of what kinds they are, how they are gained, how they are kept, why they are lost. And if ever you can find any of my fantasies pleasing, this one should not displease you; and by a prince, and especially by a new prince, it ought to be welcomed. Hence I am dedicating it to His Magnificence Giuliano [Giuliano de' Medici, the son of Lorenzo the Magnificent].[15]

Machiavelli hoped that the Medicis would read the work and understand that Machiavelli, during his 15 years of service, had gained valuable experience, had "not slept or been playing," and he was willing to accept any employment they might offer, "even if they begin by making me roll a stone."[16] Machiavelli was desperate. He hated the inactivity of his time in the country, and he feared poverty if he did not find useful employment quickly.

Machiavelli pleaded with Vettori to show *The Prince* to either Giuliano de' Medici or Pope Leo X—the two Medicis in Rome—but Vettori was unable or unwilling to help his friend. Machiavelli became increasingly anxious. By mid-1514, he was debating whether or not he should find work as a tutor. *The Prince* would one day be recognized as an important document showcasing a unique view of politics, but initially Machiavelli could not even persuade his friend of its value.

ATTEMPT TO WIN FAVOR

In the end, Machiavelli dedicated *The Prince* to Lorenzo de' Medici, Lorenzo the Magnificent's namesake and grandson, who was then in charge of all of Florence. It is clear, from the glowing language of the dedication, so distinct from the cooler, more calculating tone of the actual text, that Machiavelli was presenting this work as a kind of resume, outlining his potential value to the Medici family:

Almost always those who wish to gain a prince's favor come into his presence with such of their possessions as they hold dearest or in which they see him take most pleasure. Hence many times, princes receive as gifts horses, weapons, cloth of gold, precious stones, and similar ornaments befitting their greatness. Wishing, then, for my part to come before Your Magnificence with some proof that I am your loyal subject, I have found among my treasures nothing I hold dearer or

The courtyard of the Medici Palace, home of the ruling Medici family, is shown here. Machiavelli dedicated *The Prince* to Lorenzo de' Medici. He hoped that the Medicis would read his work and offer him employment.

value so high as my understanding of great men's actions, gained in my lengthy experience with recent matters and my continual reading on ancient ones. My observations—which with close attention I have for a long time thought over and considered, and recently have collected in a little volume—I send to Your Magnificence. And though I judge this work unworthy to come into your presence, yet I fully trust that in your kindness you will accept it, considering that I cannot make you a greater gift than to give you the means for learning, in a very short time, everything that I, in so many years and with so many troubles and perils, have discerned and comprehended. . . .

Accept this little gift, then, I beg Your Magnificence, in the spirit in which I send it; for if you consider it and read it with attention, you will discern in it my surpassing desire that you come to that greatness which Fortune and all of your own abilities promise you. And if from the summit of your lofty station, Your Magnificence ever turns your eyes to these low places, you will perceive how long I continue without desert to bear the burden of Fortune's great and steady malice.[17]

Machiavelli believed that he had a unique contribution to make. Based on his ability to bring together his realistic views and first-hand experiences with the evidence of history, he could create a set of rules that would help all leaders interested in successfully ruling a state or kingdom. Machiavelli's instructions were general and broad, but it was clear, particularly at the end of *The Prince*, that he was specifically shaping his advice to aid the Medicis.

The Prince began with an analysis of different types of princedoms—how they developed and how they were maintained. Machiavelli distinguished older, hereditary princedoms, or states, from new states, and within the section on new states, provided different advice based on whether a state had been obtained by luck, by foreign armies, by the prince's own strength and courage, by crime, or by the popular demand of the citizens.

Machiavelli included his observations of the successes and failures of Cesare Borgia. He also discussed popes, such as Julius II. He outlined the ways in which a prince might best establish his rule over a territory, to protect or increase it. He shared his thoughts on military matters, emphasizing the importance of a prince's ability to be a master of the art of war.

QUALITIES OF AN EFFECTIVE LEADER

Machiavelli's most groundbreaking thoughts came in a later section of *The Prince*, in which he cited his ideas on the qualities necessary to become a good ruler. Up until this time, most political philosophers had believed that to be a good ruler, a leader must also be a good man—by being humble, merciful, religious, steady, and honest. Machiavelli's revolutionary ideas broke with tradition. He noted that rulers, in the course of commanding a state, must often do things that would not be described as moral, that they will often find themselves facing situations in which normal moral actions would serve only to ruin the state, to endanger its safety, and to threaten its government.

Machiavelli theorized that stingy behavior could prove more effective than generosity for a leader; that cruelty might be better than kindness; that it was better for a prince to be feared than loved; and that, in many cases, keeping one's word might be dangerous. Machiavelli added, however, that it was important to keep up appearances. A prince must always seem to be very moral, even if he is not.[18]

In later chapters, Machiavelli focused on advice for a prince in choosing advisors—an opportunity for Machiavelli to insert a plug for his own services, as he suggested that the very best advisors were those who had served the previous government. Machiavelli concluded *The Prince* by specifically outlining his thoughts on why previous rulers of Italian city-states had failed to hold onto power—because they had used hired soldiers, rather than building their own army, and had alienated the common people, the noble class, or both. Machiavelli stressed the importance of a prince shaping fortune to suit him, rather than relying on fortune to always be on his side. Machiavelli noted that rulers must adjust their styles to suit the times, rather than depending on luck to keep them in power. Finally Machiavelli noted his belief that Italy was now at the perfect time for a strong prince to seize and maintain power. Given that Leo X was pope, there was clearly no one better for the job, Machiavelli suggested, than a member of Medici family, benefiting from bravery, good fortune, the support of the people of Florence, and the clear favor of God.

The Prince would establish Machiavelli as one of the leading political thinkers of the Renaissance. Sadly, however, it would fail in its obvious goal—to earn Machiavelli the favor of the Medicis and inspire them to hire him as an advisor. According to

The Prince

The Prince is recognized as one of Machiavelli's most important works, earning him a place among the great minds of the Renaissance for its revolutionary way of examining and thinking about leadership. Written mostly in 1513, it was intended as a way for Machiavelli to earn back the favor of the Medicis and inspire them to offer him a job. It would be many centuries, however, before the work marked Machiavelli as a maverick of political thought. Perhaps his most controversial ideas are those about the ideal moral conduct of leaders, as in this excerpt:

> For there is such a difference between how men live and how they ought to live that he who abandons what is done for what ought to be done learns his destruction rather than his preservation, because any man who under all conditions insists on making it his business to be good will surely be destroyed among so many who are not good. Hence a prince, in order to hold his position, must acquire the power to be not good, and understand when to use it and when not to use it in accord with necessity. . . .
>
> Is it better to be loved than feared, or the reverse? The answer is that it is desirable to be

both, but because it is difficult to join them together, it is much safer for a prince to be feared than loved, if he is to fail in one of the two. Because we can say this about men in general: they are ungrateful, changeable, simulators and dissimulators, runaways in danger, eager for gain; while you do well by them they are all yours; they offer you their blood, their property, their lives, their children . . . when need is far off; but when it comes near you, they turn about. A prince who bases himself entirely on their words, if he is lacking in other preparations, falls; because friendships gained with money, not with greatness and nobility of spirit, are purchased but not possessed, and at the right times cannot be turned to account. Men have less hesitations in injuring one who makes himself loved than one who makes himself feared, for love is held by a chain of duty which, since men are bad, they break at every chance for their own profit; but fear is held by a dread of punishment that never fails you.*

* Niccolò Machiavelli, *Machiavelli: The Chief Works and Others*, Durham, NC: Duke University Press, 1989, vol. I, pp. 57–58, 62.

one account, when Machiavelli finally did present his work to Lorenzo de' Medici, at the same time, another man had also presented Medici with a pair of racing dogs. The dogs were the gift that pleased Lorenzo de' Medici the most, and Machiavelli left in anger.[19] *The Prince* would not be published until 1532, five years after Machiavelli's death.

Test Your Knowledge

1 After being forced out of political life, what
   did Machiavelli do?
   a. He retired happily to the country
      and never thought of politics or
      Florence again.
   b. He raised an army and forced his way
      back into the city.
   c. He lived restlessly in the country until
      beginning work on *The Prince.*
   d. He began work on a book of poems
      about his experiences.

2 To whom did Machiavelli dedicate
   The Prince?
   a. Lorenzo de' Medici
   b. Pope Julius II
   c. Girolamo Savonarola
   d. The work was undedicated.

3 What contribution did Machiavelli believe
   he could make to the rulers of Florence?
   a. A large sum of money to fund their
      armies
   b. A work of art in praise of their lives
   c. A set of guidelines for successful rule
      of a kingdom
   d. None of the above

4   Prior to Machiavelli, many philosophers believed that a good ruler had to be

a. ruthless and efficient.

b. humble, religious, and honest.

c. rich.

d. well educated.

5   Which principles did Machiavelli's Prince embody?

a. Honesty and generosity

b. Religious devotion

c. Indecisiveness

d. Shrewdness and cunning

ANSWERS: 1. c; 2. a; 3. c; 4. b; 5. d

A Scholar and a Student of History

In the disappointing aftermath of *The Prince*'s completion, Machiavelli gradually began to abandon his hope of returning to an active career in politics. Instead he began to identify himself less as a diplomat, and more as a scholar, a writer, and a student of history. He joined a group of literary and historical philosophers who gathered regularly outside Florence, in the Orti Oricellari, the gardens of a palace belonging to Bernardo Rucellai, to engage in debates and scholarly discussions.

As Machiavelli began to participate more in these discussions of literature, and in the performance of plays, he decided to write a play. The result, completed around 1518, was the comedy *Mandragola*, telling the story of an elderly judge and his beautiful young wife. The play was publicly performed in Florence and Rome.

Machiavelli also began work on what would become *Discourses upon the First Decade of Titus Livius*, a three-volume political analysis of ancient and contemporary events, in which Machiavelli included his own appeal for political renewal. *Discourses* implied, in some ways, that ancient governments were superior to the ones Machiavelli had witnessed from retirement, and that Rome represented the political ideal. These themes would recur in Machiavelli's later writing.

In the preface to *Discourses*, Machiavelli began by explaining his purpose in undertaking such an ambitious task:

On account of the envious nature of men, it has always been no less dangerous to find ways and methods that are new than it has been to hunt for seas and lands unknown, since men are more prone to blame than to praise the doings of others. Nevertheless, driven by the natural eagerness I have always felt for doing without any hesitation the things that I believe will bring benefit common to everybody, I have determined to enter upon a path not yet trodden by anyone; though it may bring me trouble and difficulty, it can also bring me reward, by means of those who kindly consider the purpose of these my labors. And if my poor talents, my slight experience of present affairs, and my feeble knowledge of ancient ones make this my attempt defective and not of much use, they will at least show the way to someone who, with more vigor, more prudence and judgment, can carry out this intention of mine, which, though it may not gain me praise, ought not to bring me blame.[20]

Machiavelli continued by offering his thoughts on the value of history:

When I consider, then, how much respect is given to antiquity and how many times (to pass over countless other examples) a fragment of an antique statue has been bought at a high price in order that the buyer may have it near him, to bring reputation to his house with it, and to have it imitated by those who take pleasure in that art, and when I know that the latter then with their utmost skill attempt in all their works to imitate it, and when I see, on the other hand, that the most worthy activities which histories show us, which have been carried on in ancient kingdoms and republics by kings, generals, citizens, lawgivers, and others who have labored for their native land, are sooner admired than imitated (rather they are so much avoided by everyone in every least thing that no sign of that ancient worth remains among us), I can do no other than at the same time marvel and grieve over it. And I marvel so much the more when I see that in the differences that come up between citizens in civil affairs, or in the illnesses that men suffer from, they ever have recourse to the judgments or to the remedies that have been pronounced or prescribed by the ancients; for the civil laws are nothing else than opinions given by the ancient jurists, which, brought into order, teach our present jurists to judge. And medicine too is nothing other than the experiments made by the ancient physicians, on which present physicians base their judgments. Nonetheless, in setting up states, in maintaining governments, in ruling kingdoms, in organizing armies and managing war, in executing laws among subjects, in expanding an empire, not a single prince or republic now resorts to the examples of the ancients.[21]

Discourses was, above all else, an argument in favor of the republic form of government and, more specifically, in favor of the Roman Republic, as the apex of government. Machiavelli believed that the ancient Roman Republic offered an ideal example for contemporary Italy to follow. In *Discourses*, Machiavelli argued that the success of the Roman Republic was due to an intelligent constitution, good military structure and organization using national forces, wise planning for expansion and colonization,

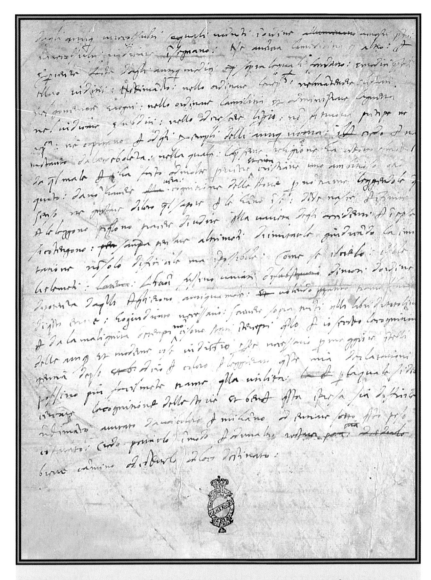

A page from Machiavelli's *Discourses upon the First Decade of Titus Livius* is shown here. The book eventually became a three-volume political analysis of ancient and contemporary events, in which Machiavelli included his own appeal for political renewal.

respect for religion and for laws, and a government based on the needs of many.

LITERARY EXPERIMENTS

Machiavelli continued to experiment with his writing, testing out different forms with which to express his ideas and his creativity. In late 1517, he began work on a poem titled *L'Asino*. Meant to serve as a kind of parody of Dante, it told the story of a man who had been transformed into a donkey, relating in flashback the events that led up to the transformation. It was not one of Machiavelli's most successful works, and was set aside after only eight chapters had been completed.

Despite its weaknesses, *L'Asino* again contained many of the same arguments Machiavelli had included in *Discourses* and *The Prince*. He suggested that politics followed a kind of cycle, in which evil follows good, and good follows evil. He was also quick to note that simple faith was not enough, that faith must be accompanied by action:

The belief that God fights for you while you are standing idle, or on your knees, has corrupted many kingdoms and many states. Prayers are certainly necessary; and he is completely insane who forbids the people their ceremonies and devotions, because from these, in truth, union and good order may be harvested; and on these, in turn, depend good and happy Fortune. But there should be no one of so little intellect, that he believes, if his house is being ruined, that God will save it without any other prop—because he will die beneath that ruin.[22]

THE ART OF WAR

By late 1520, Machiavelli had completed work on a study of the conditions that would be necessary for the type of ideal government he envisioned being established in contemporary Italy. Machiavelli believed that war was a kind of art, an art that could be taught to politicians or princes.

In *The Art of War*, Machiavelli related a conversation that allegedly took place in the Orti Oricellari, the gardens where he gathered with friends for literary and philosophical debates. According to Machiavelli, a group including several friends—and Machiavelli himself—met with a famous professional soldier named Fabrizio Colonna. Soon Colonna was expounding on the art of war, offering the Romans as the finest example of military skill. The book then turned into a series of monologues by Colonna, with the questions of the others, which were supposedly gathered that day, serving to introduce new chapters.

Machiavelli argued in *The Art of War* that there was an important connection between civilians and members of the military, that the state should have the greatest faith in men who had promised to die for its protection. Machiavelli criticized the contemporary scorn for those in the military, and noted that corruption had weakened what had been one of the most honorable professions. Finally Machiavelli argued that a politician or leader should be keenly aware of the power of the military:

> Because not the shining of precious stones and of gold maketh that the enemies submit themselves unto thee, but only the fear of the weapons; afterward, the errors which are made in other things may sometimes be corrected, but those which are done in the war—the pain straight way coming on—cannot be amended.[23]

RESTORED TO GRACE

Machiavelli's continued efforts to win favor with the Medicis began to meet some small measure of success after the death of Lorenzo de' Medici, on May 4, 1519. Just three years earlier, Lorenzo de' Medici had taken the title of Duke of Urbino, becoming the first member of the Medici family to take a royal title in order to cement his rule over Florence. He no longer cloaked his ambitions by assuming no title and governing as a kind of private citizen. Lorenzo de' Medici had no sons—he had only an infant daughter, Catherine—so his uncle, Cardinal Giulio de' Medici, was sent back to Florence by Pope Leo X to maintain Medici control over Florence after Lorenzo's death.

Cardinal Giulio was more approachable than other members of the Medici family. Once again, Machiavelli asked his friends to intercede on his behalf with the new ruler of Florence. Battista della Palla, one of Machiavelli's literary friends, met with the pope in April 1520 to present Machiavelli's case. The result, he informed Machiavelli, was that the pope was "very well disposed toward you," and the pope had suggested to the cardinal that Machiavelli

Giovanni de' Medici became Pope Leo X. The pope, shown here leading a procession through Florence, looked favorably upon Machiavelli's writing. The pope's favor would eventually lead to a new writing commission for Machiavelli.

should be used in some way, perhaps by commissioning him to do some "writing or something else."[24]

Machiavelli's first official mission in years, however, would not involve writing or high-level diplomacy. Instead Cardinal Giulio asked him to oversee the bankruptcy case of a merchant in Lucca. Machiavelli's task was to meet with the political authorities in Lucca and negotiate an honorable settlement of the merchant's debts to other merchants in Florence, to whom he owed large sums of money.

Such a mission was a considerable letdown for the man who had once traveled as an official representative of Florence, meeting with kings, but

Contract for *History of Florence*

On November 8, 1520, Machiavelli's commission to write *History of Florence* was approved. The commission was officially issued on behalf of the University of Pisa, whose commissioner, Francesco del Nero, was charged with formalizing the contract. The commission did, however, have the Medici stamp of approval. The agreement had been made at the request of Cardinal Giulio de' Medici who, three years after the commission was approved, would become Pope Clement VII.

Machiavelli himself drafted the contract agreement, leaving blanks for the period in which the contract would be in force and the payment (later set at 100 florins):

Machiavelli wanted to return to a government position, no matter how small. So he accepted the commission and took advantage of his time in Lucca to make notes on the government there.

When he returned to Florence, a better opportunity awaited. His friend Battista della Palla had returned from Rome with news that the Medici family was funding a writing project—to relate the

---

To his honored brother-in-law, Francesco del Nero

Honored Sir:

The substance of the contract will be this:

He is to be hired for _____ years with an annual salary of _____, with the obligation that he must and will be held to write the annals or history of the things done by the state and city of Florence, beginning with the date that seems to him suitable, and in that language—whether Latin or Tuscan—that seems to him best.*

Niccolò Machiavelli

* Allan Gilbert, ed. *The Letters of Machiavelli*. New York: Capricorn Books, 1961, p. 197.

history of Florence—and Machiavelli had been selected as its author. On November 8, 1520, the commission was approved. Machiavelli was to receive 100 florins for the project, approximately half of what he had earned as secretary many years before. Machiavelli accepted gratefully the opportunity to become a historian of Florence.

Test Your Knowledge

1 After giving up on any possible return to active political life, what did Machiavelli do?

a. He became a scholar and historian.

b. He joined a group of literary philosophers.

c. He composed a play.

d. All of the above

2 Machiavelli's *Discourses* extols the virtues of

a. the Medici family.

b. the Roman Republic.

c. life in exile.

d. the Catholic Church.

3 What is the subject of Machiavelli's unfinished poem, *L'Asino*?

a. A man transformed into a donkey

b. An angel that visits earth

c. Lorenzo de' Medici

d. A traveling musician

4 In *The Art of War*, Machiavelli argues that

a. a leader should never trust his soldiers.

b. wars are best fought by cunning and deception.

c. the power of the military is precious and should be respected.

d. none of the above.

5   Machiavelli returned to public life as
    a. Duke of Urbino.
    b. a lawyer in Florence.
    c. author of an official history of Florence.
    d. a judge.

ANSWERS: 1. d; 2. b; 3. a; 4. c; 5. c

History of Florence

For nearly the rest of his life, Machiavelli would dedicate himself to researching and writing *History of Florence*. It would prove to be his longest work, and would provide an opportunity for him to revisit some of his most cherished political philosophies.

Machiavelli's commission as historian of Florence put him in a somewhat awkward position. He had been hired to write the history of Florence by a member of the Medici family, a family that had dominated Florence's politics—sometimes in brutal and unjust ways—for many generations. Machiavelli needed to relate Florence's history without focusing too intensely on the ways and means by which the Medicis had seized and retained power.

Initially Machiavelli intended to begin his *History of Florence* with the year 1434, the year in which Cosimo de' Medici began the rise to power of a family that would dominate Florence for much of the next century. Machiavelli changed his plans, however, needing, he believed, to more accurately outline Florence's past through a study of the civil divisions and dissent that had shaped the city's early history.

The first four books of *History* contain an exploration of Florence's past, beginning with a broad outline of Italian history, and continuing with the gradual transformation of Florence, the divisions of its people, and the eventual rise to power of the Medici family. The fifth and sixth books focus

The eighth and final book of Machiavelli's *History of Florence* details the reign of Lorenzo de' Medici, who died in 1492. The tomb of Lorenzo de' Medici is shown here.

little on Florence, detailing instead the frequent wars between Italian city-states. The seventh book details Florence's history from 1427 until 1464, focusing intensely on the life and accomplishments of the patron of the Medici family, Cosimo de'

Medici. The eighth and final book details the reign of Lorenzo the Magnificent, containing extensive coverage of the attempt to assassinate him and the war that followed. This last book concludes with a dire warning about Italy's decay and loss of power.

Instead of providing an extensive and comprehensive history of Florence, Machiavelli's work provided a platform for his political theories. The speeches included in the history may or may not actually have been made, as he cited. In some instances, it seems clear that the words were fiction, created to better illustrate a particular point.

Machiavelli's ideas were most clearly expressed in the preface to each book. Once more, the key themes of his philosophy emerged: the comparison between ancient and modern styles of government and military operations, the purpose of war, the reasons for the rise and fall of republics, and the nature of corruption. Once more, Machiavelli expanded upon his theory that politics and government exist in a kind of cycle—that the rise of a power to its highest level is always followed by a decline. Evil always follows good, and good follows evil.

The real theme of *History of Florence* was this idea of cycles, the sense that states fell into decline, rose, and then declined again. Machiavelli's interest was not in a simple reporting of the history of these cycles, but in gaining an understanding of why they occurred. Specifically, Machiavelli wanted to provide the reader with a sense of why states became corrupt and, perhaps more importantly, how Florence—and all of Italy—had been corrupted, and how they could be revitalized.

For Machiavelli, the study of the princes of Italy did not inspire the same admiration and respect as the study of the ancient rulers of Rome. He did not perceive the same bravery, or the same sense of patriotic duty. Instead, in Machiavelli's view, the more recent Italian rulers offered a history of deceit and fraud, attempts by princes and politicians to maintain a reputation they never earned, and evidence of a weakened military unable to keep the land safe from invaders.[25]

These are strong words from an author who owed his commission to a member of the Medici family. Yet Machiavelli was equally critical of Florence itself, charging that it was hopelessly corrupt and

The *History of Florence*

Machiavelli's *History of Florence*, written over
four and a half years, offered a platform for
Machiavelli to outline his political theories in the
context of his native city's history. In the opening of
the second book, he details his theory that colonization
is a critical component to the security of a government:

> One of the great and wonderful provisions of
> ancient republics and principalities which in
> these present times has vanished, was that for
> building at all times numbers of new cities and
> towns. Nothing is so worthy of an excellent
> prince or of a well-organized republic or so
> useful to a province as to build new towns
> where men can gather for convenient defense
> and farming. This the ancients could easily
> bring about through their habit of sending into
> conquered or empty countries new inhabitants
> whom they called colonies. Not only was this
> practice the cause for building new cities but it
> made a conquered province more secure for the
> conqueror, filled empty places with inhabitants,
> and kept men well distributed within the
> provinces. As a result of this process, since men
> lived more comfortably in such a province, they
> increased in number there and in attack were
> speedier and in defense more secure.

Since this custom, through the bad practice of republics and princes, has now vanished, its disuse causes the ruin and weakness of provinces, for only this method makes empires more secure and, as I have said, keeps countries thickly inhabited. Security results because a colony that a prince places in a newly conquered land is like a castle and a garrison to hold the others in loyalty. Without this, he cannot keep a province fully inhabited or make sure that the population is well distributed, because all the places in it are not productive or healthful. For this reason, there are in some places plenty of men but in others they are scarce; and if there is no way for taking them for where they are plentiful and putting them where they are scarce, a province in a short time is ruined, for one part of it, through its small number of inhabitants, becomes desert, and another, through their excess, becomes poor. And because nature cannot provide for this defect, diligence must provide for it. Countries that are unhealthful become healthful when a multitude of men all at once takes possession; for with cultivation they give health to the ground and with fires they cleanse the air—something Nature could never provide for.*

* Niccolò Machiavelli, *Machiavelli: The Chief Works and Others.* Durham, NC: Duke University Press, 1989, vol. III, pp. 1080–1081.

suggesting that few forms of government could hope for success because of what Machiavelli pinpointed as the greatest evil—a hopelessly weakened and ineffective military structure. As he noted in the beginning of the sixth book:

> Ancient and well-ordered republics, as the result of their [military] victories, usually filled their treasuries with silver and gold, distributed gifts to the people, remitted tribute to their subjects, and with games and splendid shows entertained them. But victories in the times we are describing first emptied the treasury and then impoverished the people, and from your enemies they did not protect you.[26]

History of Florence ended with the death of Lorenzo the Magnificent, in 1492. Machiavelli planned to write additional books, to bring the history up to date, but he was unable to do so. The Medici who had commissioned the work—Cardinal Giulio de' Medici—had been chosen as the new pope, Clement VII. He was impressed by *History*, giving Machiavelli additional financial support and seeking his advice for a plan to create his own papal

Giulio de' Medici, who became Pope Clement VII, is shown here with Charles V. The pope was impressed by Machiavelli's *History*, eventually giving Machiavelli additional financial support and seeking his advice in his plan to create his own papal militia.

militia. The pope gradually lost interest, however, and after spending some time in Rome, Machiavelli returned to Florence.

RETURN TO POLITICS

Machiavelli included in both *History of Florence* and *Discourses* examples of how popes had contributed to the weakening of Italy. Yet, ironically, Machiavelli, eager to return to politics, had been willing to assist the pope in his efforts to create a papal militia.

Machiavelli's reputation was restored by the successful reception of *History of Florence* and by the support of the pope. He was, once again, busy with official assignments, including a mission to Venice in August 1525. In May 1526, he was elected to a commission investigating systems for providing Florence with better fortification in the event of an attack. Machiavelli quickly busied himself with drafting lengthy recommendations, which were well received, but produced no real results.

Machiavelli was fortunate to have been restored to the good graces of the Medicis. Their time in power, however, would soon come to an end. In May 1527, Spanish-German forces swept through Italy and attacked Rome, seizing the city. Pope Clement VII was forced into hiding, and eventually fled Rome, as the city was ransacked by foreign soldiers. With the collapse of the pope's authority in Rome, opponents to the Medicis in Florence overthrew the government and restored the republic. Machiavelli, who, after 15 years, had finally won

In May 1527, German forces swept through Italy and attacked Rome, seizing the city. Pope Clement VII was forced into hiding, and eventually fled Rome, as the city was ransacked by foreign soldiers.

back a political role in the Medici government, was again unemployed—this time a victim of his ties to the Medicis.

Machiavelli had little time to appreciate the irony of this latest twist of fate, or to attempt to win the support of the new government. On June 21, 1527, less than two weeks after the election of a new government in Florence, Niccolò Machiavelli was dead, the result of an illness he had contracted soon after he reached Florence.

LEGACY OF A RADICAL THINKER

After Machiavelli's death, as more of his writings came to light and shocked contemporary readers, his reputation as a radical and controversial political theorist began to take shape. Most of this acclaim was due to the posthumous publication of *The Prince*, which earned its author a reputation that would, no doubt, have amused him. Shakespeare would cite him as "the murderous Machiavel," and philosopher Edmund Burke would describe the French Revolution as bearing evidence of the "odious maxims of a Machiavellian policy."[27] In the sixteenth and seventeenth centuries, Machiavelli was described as a tool of Satan, as "the great muster-master of hell."[28] His very name had become synonymous with evil, sinister, and unscrupulous behavior.

Machiavelli liked to surprise and shock his readers. He was aware that some of his political ideas were unconventional and revolutionary. He sought to make a reputation for himself, not by stating the obvious, or relating history in a straightforward, orderly manner, but by shaping history to suit his theories, by reversing traditional ideas of leadership and government.

Machiavelli's life and all of his writings reveal a complicated picture—a man eager to return to active political life, a civil servant desperate to prove his usefulness to a new regime, an observer of leaders interested in sharing his observations of what made and unmade a strong ruler. Machiavelli knew—from bitter, firsthand experience—how rapidly power could shift from one form of government to another. He had met with leaders at the height of their power, and witnessed them when fortune had abandoned them.

His ideas were shaped by the politics of Florence in the fifteenth and sixteenth centuries, and by his years of study of ancient history. He was not, by choice, a remote, objective observer of historical events. Instead he eagerly engaged in diplomacy and political debate, and preferred a public role to actively translate his ideas into actions and policies.

Machiavelli's aim was not to advance the career of a single man or government. He was willing to adapt to different regimes, to different times, and he believed that skilled leaders should do the same. Instead his aim was to preserve Florence or, perhaps more accurately, to restore Florence to its former glory. He sought to sweep away the corruption that he believed was at the root of its decline, to provide it with a strong military, to ensure that its leaders modeled themselves on the great rulers of ancient times. "I love my native city more than my own soul," he wrote near the end of his life.[29]

Machiavelli offered to the rulers of Florence what he viewed as his greatest gift—his recipe for ideal leadership, intended to provide Florence with strong and stable governments. His efforts failed. Florence would never recapture the greatness it had experienced during the early years of the Renaissance, but Machiavelli's ideas outlived the men for whom they were intended. For more than 500 years, his writings have offered a compelling,

controversial philosophy of leadership, and a fasci-
nating glimpse into the life of a man whose political
theories sought to restore his native city to a place
of honor and glory.

Test Your Knowledge

1 What was Machiavelli's longest work?
   a. *The Prince*
   b. *The Art of War*
   c. *History of Florence*
   d. *Discourses upon the First Decade of Titus Livius*

2 Machiavelli's historical texts reflect which of the following ideas?
   a. That God is the ultimate judge of all human action
   b. That political power follows an eternal cycle of rise and fall
   c. That all men are basically good at heart
   d. None of the above

3 Machiavelli's return to public life was cut short by what event?
   a. The death of the pope
   b. An earthquake
   c. The invasion of Italy by German and Spanish forces
   d. The economic collapse of central Europe

4 Later authors and philosophers characterized Machiavelli as
   a. murderous.
   b. obnoxious.
   c. a tool of Satan.
   d. all of the above.

5 In reviewing the sum of Machiavelli's work, his *chief* aim had been

a. to create a plan for leadership that would restore Florence to greatness.

b. to encourage corrupt, power-mad leaders.

c. to impress the Medici family.

d. to gain a place in history.

ANSWERS: 1. c; 2. b; 3. c; 4. d; 5. a

1469 Machiavelli is born in Florence on May 3.

1478 Lorenzo de' Medici survives an assassination attempt while attending Mass at the Duomo.

1489 Girolamo Savonarola begins preaching sermons denouncing the Medicis.

1492 Lorenzo de' Medici dies.

1494 Piero de' Medici signs a peace treaty with the invading French army, and is then forced to flee Florence; sixty-year reign of Medicis in Florence comes to an end; Florence becomes a republic.

1500 Machiavelli travels to France to meet with King Louis XII

1469 Machiavelli is born in Florence on May 3

1506 Machiavelli is sent on mission to Pope Julius II

1460

1502 Machiavelli negotiates with Cesare Borgia

1498 Machiavelli begins work as head of Second Chancery

1498   Savonarola is hanged; Machiavelli becomes head of the Second Chancery and secretary of the Ten of War.

1499   Machiavelli accepts his first diplomatic missions on behalf of Jacopo d'Appiano and Caterina Sforza.

1500   Machiavelli travels to France to meet with King Louis XII.

1501   Machiavelli marries Marietta Corsini.

1502   Machiavelli meets Cesare Borgia.

1503   Machiavelli is sent to Rome to witness the naming of a new pope, Julius II.

1520   Machiavelli completes *The Art of War*; receives commission to write *History of Florence*

1512   Florentine Republic is overthrown; Machiavelli loses job

1527   Medici government is overthrown; Machiavelli dies on June 21

1530

1525   Machiavelli is sent on diplomatic mission to Venice

1513 Machiavelli is arrested and imprisoned; later writes *The Prince*

1506 Machiavelli completes training and organization of Florence's militia; negotiates with Pope Julius II.

1507 Machiavelli meets with Emperor Maximilian.

1512 Holy League armies overwhelm Prato; Florentine Republic is overthrown; Medicis return; Machiavelli loses his job on November 7.

1513 Machiavelli is arrested and imprisoned under suspicion of plotting the overthrow of the Medicis; he is finally released on March 12; he writes *The Prince*.

1516 Machiavelli begins work on *Discourses upon the First Decade of Titus Livius*.

1520 Machiavelli completes *The Art of War*; wins support of Cardinal Giulio de' Medici; is granted commission to write *History of Florence*.

1525 Machiavelli is sent on a diplomatic mission to Venice.

1526 Machiavelli is elected to fortification commission.

1527 Spanish-German forces attack Rome, forcing pope into hiding; Medici government is overthrown; Machiavelli loses job; dies on June 21.

NOTES

CHAPTER 1
Portrait of a Political Philosopher

1. Quentin Skinner, *Machiavelli*. New York: Hill and Wang, 1981, pp. 87–88.

2. Niccolò Machiavelli, *The Prince*. New York: Penguin Books, 1981, p. 134.

3. Ibid., p. 29.

4. James B. Atkinson and David Sices, eds. *Machiavelli and His Friends: Their Personal Correspondence*. Dekalb, IL: Northern Illinois University Press, 1996, p. 135.

CHAPTER 2
Early Years in Florence

5. Niccolò Machiavelli, *Machiavelli: The Chief Works and Others*. Durham, NC: Duke University Press, 1989, vol. I, p. 47.

6. Maurizio Viroli, *Niccolò's Smile: A Biography of Machiavelli*. New York: Farrar, Straus and Giroux, 2000, p. 25.

CHAPTER 3
Diplomatic Career

7. Quentin Skinner, *Machiavelli: A Very Short Introduction*. New York: Oxford University Press, 2000, p. 7.

8. Viroli, *Niccolò's Smile: A Biography of Machiavelli,* p. 51.

9. Skinner, *Machiavelli: A Very Short Introduction,* p. 10.

10. Machiavelli, *Legations 13.74,* in *Machiavelli: The Chief Works and Others,* vol. 1, p. 160.

CHAPTER 4
Decline of the Republic

11. Viroli, *Niccolò's Smile: A Biography of Machiavelli,* p. 94.

12. Machiavelli, *The Prince,* in *Machiavelli: The Chief Works and Others,* vol. 1, p. 87.

13. Viroli, *Niccolò's Smile: A Biography of Machiavelli,* p. 113.

14. Allan Gilbert, ed., *The Letters of Machiavelli*. New York: Capricorn Books, 1961, pp. 100–101.

CHAPTER 5
The Prince

15. Gilbert, *The Letters of Machiavelli,* pp. 142–143.

16. Ibid., p. 144.

17. Machiavelli, *Machiavelli: The Chief Works and Others,* vol. 1, pp. 10–11.

18. Sydney Anglo, *Machiavelli: A Dissection*. New York: Harcourt, Brace & World, 1969, p. 72.

19. Ibid., p. 81.

CHAPTER 6
A Scholar and a Student of History

20. Machiavelli, *Machiavelli: The Chief Works and Others,* vol. 1, p. 190.

21. Ibid., pp. 190–191.
22. Anglo, *Machiavelli: A Dissection,* p. 118.
23. Viroli, *Niccolò's Smile: A Biography of Machiavelli,* p. 192.
24. Anglo, *Machiavelli: A Dissection,* p. 144.

CHAPTER 7
History of Florence
25. Anglo, *Machiavelli: A Dissection,* p. 176.

26. Machiavelli, *Machiavelli: The Chief Works and Others,* vol. III, p. 1284.
27. Skinner, *Machiavelli: A Very Short Introduction,* p. 1.
28. Anglo, *Machiavelli: A Dissection,* p. 271.
29. Gilbert, *The Letters of Machiavelli,* p. 249.

Anglo, Sydney. *Machiavelli: A Dissection.* New York: Harcourt, Brace & World, 1969.

Atkinson, James B. and David Sices. *Machiavelli and His Friends: Their Personal Correspondence.* Dekalb, IL: Northern Illinois University Press, 1996.

Burke, Peter. *The Italian Renaissance: Culture and Society in Italy.* Princeton, NJ: Princeton University Press, 1986.

Gilbert, Allan, ed. *The Letters of Machiavelli.* New York: Capricorn Books, 1961.

Machiavelli, Niccolò. *Machiavelli: The Chief Works and Others,* volumes I-III. Durham, NC: Duke University Press, 1989.

———. *The Prince.* New York: Penguin Books, 1981.

Plumb, J.H., ed. *Renaissance Profiles.* New York: Harper & Row Publishers, 1961.

Ridolfi, Roberto. *The Life of Niccolò Machiavelli.* Chicago: The University of Chicago Press, 1963.

Skinner, Quentin. *Machiavelli.* New York: Hill and Wang, 1981.

———. *Machiavelli: A Very Short Introduction.* New York: Oxford University Press, 2000.

Villari, Pasquale. *The Life and Times of Niccolò Machiavelli.* New York: Charles Scribner's Sons, 1914.

Viroli, Maurizio. *Niccolò's Smile: A Biography of Machiavelli.* New York: Farrar, Straus and Giroux, 2000.

Books

Machiavelli, Niccolò. *The Art of War.* Cambridge, MA: Da Capo Press, 2001.

———. *The Prince.* New York: Penguin Books, 1981.

Plumb, J.H., ed. *Renaissance Profiles.* New York: Harper & Row Publishers, 1961.

Skinner, Quentin. *Machiavelli: A Very Short Introduction.* New York: Oxford University Press, 2000.

Websites

The History Guide: Lectures on Modern European Intellectual History Nicolò Machiavelli (1429–1527)
http://www.historyguide.org/intellect/machiavelli.html

The Internet Encyclopedia of Philosophy: Nicolò Machiavelli (1429–1527)
http://www.utm.edu/research/iep/m/machiave.htm

PBS: The Medicis
www.pbs.org/empires/medici/

The Prince, by Nicolò Machiavelli
www.constitution.org/mac/prince00.htm

page:
3: © SEF/Art Resource, NY
5: © Alinari/Art Resource, NY
8: © Erich Lessing/Art Resource, NY
22: © Scala/Art Resource, NY
26: © Scala/Art Resource, NY
29: © Summerfield Press/ CORBIS
37: © Scala/Art Resource, NY
41: © Bettmann/CORBIS
49: © Archivo Iconographico, S.A./ CORBIS

61: © Archivo Iconographico, S.A./ CORBIS
63: © Scala/Art Resource, NY
67: © Bettmann/CORBIS
77: © Erich Lessing/Art Resource, NY
81: © Scala/Art Resource, NY
96: © Scala/Art Resource, NY
101: © Scala/Art Resource, NY
109: © Scala/Art Resource, NY
115: © Scala/Art Resource, NY
117: © Bettmann/CORBIS

Cover: © Scala/Art Resource, NY

Heather Lehr Wagner is a writer and an editor. She is the author of more than 30 books exploring social and political issues and focusing on the lives of prominent men and women. She earned a B.A. in political science from Duke University, and an M.A. in government from the College of William and Mary. She lives with her husband and family in Pennsylvania.